BRITISH RAILWAYS STEAMING ON THE LONDON MIDLAND REGION

Volume Three

Compiled by
PETER HANDS & COLIN RICHARDS

DEFIANT PUBLICATIONS
190 Yoxall Road,
Shirley, Solihull,
West Midlands.

Printed in Europe by the Gorenjski Tisk printing house — Kranj, Yugoslavia.

CURRENT STEAM PHOTOGRAPH ALBUMS AVAILABLE FROM DEFIANT PUBLICATIONS

VOLUME 3
A4 size - Hardback. 100 pages
-182 b/w photographs.
£7.95 + 75p postage.
ISBN 0 946857 02 4.

VOLUME 4
A4 size - Hardback. 100 pages
-182 b/w photographs.
£7.95 + 75p postage.
ISBN 0 946857 04 0.

VOLUME 5
A4 size - Hardback. 100 pages
-180 b/w photographs.
£7.95 + 75p postage.
ISBN 0 946857 06 7.

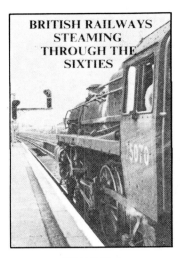

VOLUME 6
A4 size - Hardback. 100 pages
-182 b/w photographs.
£8.45 + 75p postage.
ISBN 0 946857 08 3.

VOLUME 7
A4 size - Hardback. 100 pages
-182 b/w photographs.
£8.45 + 75p postage.
ISBN 0 946857 10 5.

VOLUME 8
A4 size - Hardback. 100 pages
-181 b/w photographs.
£8.95 + 75p postage.
ISBN 0 946857 14 8.

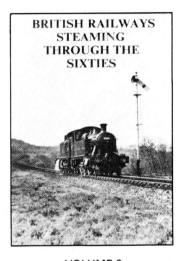

VOLUME 9
A4 size - Hardback. 100 pages
-182 b/w photographs.
£9.95 + 75p postage.
ISBN 0 946857 18 0.

VOLUME 10
A4 size - Hardback. 100 pages
-182 b/w photographs.
£9.95 + 75p postage.
ISBN 0 946857 20 2.

VOLUME 11
A4 size - Hardback. 100 pages
-180 b/w photographs.
£10.95 + 75p postage.
ISBN 0 946857 24 5.

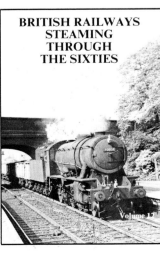

VOLUME 12
A4 size - Hardback. 100 pages
-182 b/w photographs.
£11.95 + 75p postage.
ISBN 0 946857 27 X.

VOLUME 1
A4 size - Hardback. 100 pages
-187 b/w photographs.
£9.95 + 75p postage.
ISBN 0 946857 19 9.

BRITISH RAILWAYS
STEAMING ON
THE EX-LNER
LINES

IN
PREPARATION

VOLUME 2

CURRENT STEAM PHOTOGRAPH ALBUMS AVAILABLE
FROM DEFIANT PUBLICATIONS

BRITISH RAILWAYS STEAMING THROUGH THE FIFTIES

VOLUME 1
A4 size - Hardback. 100 pages
-18/ b/w photographs.
£8.95 + 75p postage.
ISBN 0 946857 12 1.

BRITISH RAILWAYS STEAMING THROUGH THE FIFTIES

VOLUME 2
A4 size - Hardback. 100 pages
-180 b/w photographs.
£8.95 + 75p postage.
ISBN 0 946857 13 X.

BRITISH RAILWAYS STEAMING THROUGH THE FIFTIES

VOLUME 3
A4 size - Hardback. 100 pages
-180 b/w photographs.
£9.95 + 75p postage.
ISBN 0 946857 16 4.

BRITISH RAILWAYS STEAMING THROUGH THE FIFTIES

VOLUME 4
A4 size - Hardback. 100 pages
-180 b/w photographs.
£9.95 + 75p postage.
ISBN 0 946857 17 2.

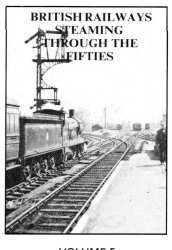

BRITISH RAILWAYS STEAMING THROUGH THE FIFTIES

VOLUME 5
A4 size - Hardback. 100 pages
-180 b/w photographs.
£9.95 + 75p postage.
ISBN 0 946857 22 9.

BRITISH RAILWAYS STEAMING THROUGH THE FIFTIES

VOLUME 6
A4 size - Hardback. 100 pages
-180 b/w photographs.
£9.95 + 75p postage.
ISBN 0 946857 23 7.

BRITISH RAILWAYS STEAMING THROUGH THE FIFTIES

VOLUME 7
IN PREPARATION
NOVEMBER 1990

BRITISH RAILWAYS STEAMING THROUGH THE FIFTIES

VOLUME 8
IN
PREPARATION
NOVEMBER 1990

BRITISH RAILWAYS STEAMING ON THE WESTERN REGION

VOLUME 1
A4 size - Hardback. 100 pages
-188 b/w photographs.
£7.95 + 75p postage.
ISBN 0 946857 03 2.

BRITISH RAILWAYS STEAMING ON THE WESTERN REGION

VOLUME 2
A4 size - Hardback. 100 pages
-181 b/w photographs.
£8.45 + 75p postage.
ISBN 0 946857 11 3.

BRITISH RAILWAYS STEAMING ON THE WESTERN REGION

VOLUME 3
A4 size - Hardback. 100 pages
-179 b/w photographs.
£10.95 + 75p postage.
ISBN 0 946857 25 3.

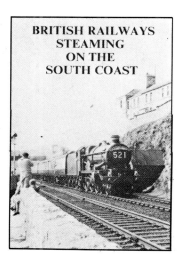

BRITISH RAILWAYS STEAMING ON THE SOUTH COAST

IN
PREPARATION
NOVEMBER 1990

CURRENT STEAM PHOTOGRAPH ALBUMS AVAILABLE FROM DEFIANT PUBLICATIONS

BRITISH RAILWAYS STEAMING ON THE LONDON MIDLAND REGION

VOLUME 1
A4 size - Hardback. 100 pages -184 b/w photographs.
£7.95 + 75p postage.
ISBN 0 946857 05 9.

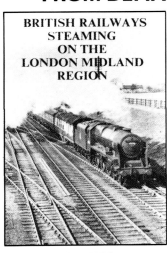

BRITISH RAILWAYS STEAMING ON THE LONDON MIDLAND REGION

VOLUME 2
A4 size - Hardback. 100 pages -181 b/w photographs.
£8.95 + 75p postage.
ISBN 0 946857 15 6.

BRITISH RAILWAYS STEAMING ON THE LONDON MIDLAND REGION

VOLUME 3
A4 size - Hardback. 100 pages -181 b/w photographs.
£11.95 + 75p postage.
ISBN 0 946857 28 8.

BRITISH RAILWAYS STEAMING ON THE EAST COAST MAIN LINE

A4 size - Hardback. 100 pages -183 b/w photographs.
£8.95 + 75p postage.
ISBN 0 946857 07 5.
(Reprinted July 1988)

BRITISH RAILWAYS STEAMING ON THE SOUTHERN REGION

VOLUME 1
A4 size - Hardback. 100 pages -188 b/w photographs.
£8.95 + 75p postage.
ISBN 0 946857 09 1.

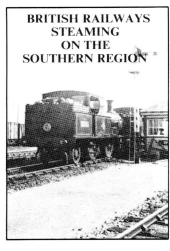

BRITISH RAILWAYS STEAMING ON THE SOUTHERN REGION

VOLUME 2
A4 size - Hardback. 100 pages -181 b/w photographs.
£9.95 + 75p postage.
ISBN 0 946857 21 0.

BRITISH RAILWAYS STEAMING ON THE SOUTHERN REGION

IN PREPARATION

VOLUME 3

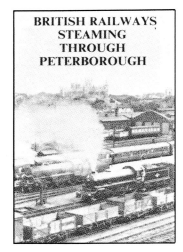

BRITISH RAILWAYS STEAMING THROUGH PETERBOROUGH

A4 size - Hardback. 100 pages -163 b/w photographs.
£10.95 + 75p postage.
ISBN 0 946857 26 1.

OTHER TITLES AVAILABLE FROM DEFIANT PUBLICATIONS
PRICES VARY FROM £1 to £3.80 INCLUDING POSTAGE

WHAT HAPPENED TO STEAM

This series of booklets, 50 in all, is designed to inform the reader of the allocations, re-allocations and dates of withdrawal of steam locomotives during their last years of service. From 1957 onwards and finally where the locomotives concerned were stored and subsequently scrapped.

BR STEAMSHED ALLOCATIONS

This series lists individual steam locomotives based at the different parent depots of B. R. from January 1957 until each depot either closed to steam or closed completely. An attractive bookbinder is available for this thirteen book series.

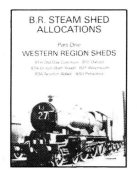

ACKNOWLEDGEMENTS

Grateful thanks are extended to the following contributors of photographs not only for their use in this book but for their kind patience and long term loan of negatives/ photographs whilst this book was being compiled.

T. R. AMOS TAMWORTH	ALAN BAILEY LEEDS	BRIAN BENNETT BURGESS HILL
B. W. L. BROOKSBANK LONDON	N. L. BROWNE ALDERSHOT	R. BUTTERFIELD MIRFIELD
CHRISTOPHER FIFIELD LONDON	A. N. H. GLOVER BIRMINGHAM	J. D. GOMERSALL SHEFFIELD
T. HAILES OULTON BROAD	D. HARRISON CHAPELTOWN	PETER HAY HOVE
M. F. HIGSON THE SMOKEBOX	R. W. HINTON GLOUCESTER	
H. L. HOLLAND ST. CATHERINES, ONTARIO, CANADA		A. C. INGRAM WISBECH
D. K. JONES MOUNTAIN ASH	B. J. MILLER BARRY	A. F. NISBET BRACKLEY
C. J. PERKINS NOTTINGHAM	R. PICTON WOLVERHAMPTON	W. POTTER BISHOPS CLEEVE
N. E. PREEDY HUCCLECOTE	P. A. ROWLINGS ALCONBURY	K. L. SEAL ANDOVERSFORD
G. W. SHARPE BARNSLEY	C. P. STACEY STONY STRATFORD	M. S. STOKES MARPLE
JOHN STONES TUNBRIDGE WELLS	A. SWAIN WEMBLEY	MIKE TURNER BROAD HINTON
TERRY WARD NORTHAMPTON	G. H. WILSON BIRMINGHAM	KIT WINDLE LOWER BREDBURY
MIKE WOOD BIRMINGHAM	T. WRIGHT SLOUGH	

Front Cover — 6G Llandudno Junction "Caprotti" Class 5 4—6—0 No 44740 accelerates out of Colwyn Bay station, at the start of its journey with the 11.00 am express to Manchester (W480) on 11th September 1954. No 44740 remained at Llandudno Junction shed until withdrawn in April 1963.

(N. L. Browne)

ISBN 0 946857 28 8

© P. B. HANDS/C. RICHARDS 1990
FIRST PUBLISHED 1990

INTRODUCTION

BRITISH RAILWAYS STEAMING ON THE LONDON MIDLAND REGION — Volume Three, is the third book to concentrate on the London Midland Region from the "British Railways Steaming Through The Fifties and Sixties" stable. Unlike the earlier two albums Scotland is not represented as a "BR STEAMING ON THE SCOTTISH REGION" album is planned for release in 1991.

These books are designed to give the ordinary, everyday steam photographic enthusiast of the 1950's and 1960's a chance to participate in and give pleasure to others whilst recapturing the twilight days of steam.

Apart from the main series, further individual albums will be produced from time to time. Wherever possible, no famous names will be found nor will photographs which have been published before be used. Nevertheless, the content and quality of the majority of photographs selected will be second to none.

This third album contains a wide and varied selection of photographs of steam at work and rest from many different locations on the London Midland Region from 1948—1968 when allocated steam finished. Unless otherwise stated all locomotives are of LMS origin.

The majority of the photographs used in this album have been contributed by readers of Peter Hands series of booklets entitled "What Happened To Steam" and "BR Steam Shed Allocations" and from readers of the earlier "BR Steaming Through The Sixties" albums. Under normal circumstances these may have been hidden from the public eye for ever.

The continuation of the "BR Steaming" series etc., depends upon you the reader. If you feel you have suitable material of BR steam locomotives between 1948—1968 and wish to contribute them towards this series and other future publications please contact either:

Peter Hands,
190 Yoxall Road,
Shirley, Solihull,
West Midlands B90 3RN

OR

Colin Richards,
28 Kendrick Close,
Damson Parkway, Solihull,
West Midlands B92 OQD

Pete Hands

CONTENTS

NAMEPLATES — Some example nameplates of Ex. L. M. S. locomotives

1) Unrebuilt *Patriot* Class 4-6-0 No 45543 *Home Guard.* (N. E. Preedy)

2) *Jubilee* Class 4-6-0 No 45569 *Tasmania.* (N. E. Preedy)

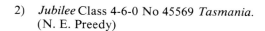

3) *Royal Scot* Class 4-6-0 No 46136 *The Border Regiment.* (C. J. Perkins)

4) *Princess* Class 4-6-2 No 46200 *The Princess Royal.* (N. E. Preedy)

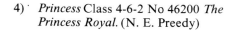

5) *Coronation* Class 4-6-2 No 46240 *City of Coventry.* (N. E. Preedy)

PLATFORM
1

6) Journey's end for *Princess* Class 4-6-2 No 46200 *The Princess Royal*, from 8A Edge Hill (Liverpool) as it rests near to the buffer stops at Euston, after arrival with the up *Merseyside Express* from Liverpool (Lime Street), whilst a group of gentlemen attempt to sort out their luggage on Platform One — circa 1958. Observe the cast iron columns supporting the curving roof, long since swept away by modernisation. (M. F. Higson — The Smokebox)

7)   Stanier Class 8F 2-8-0 No 48603, a 1A Willesden locomotive, finds itself at work on an up Class 6 freight train as it lays a trail of black smoke, north of Loughborough on the former Midland main line on 11th April 1964. Upon the closure of Willesden to steam in September 1965, No 48603 was transferred to the Midlands, serving at 2F Bescot and 2E Saltley before moving on to 6A Chester in March 1967. (K. L. Seal)

8)   For many years a regular performer from Blackpool shed on these trains, *Jubilee* Class 4-6-0 No 45574 *India* approaches Leyland with the 10.15 am limited stop from Blackpool (Central) to Manchester (Victoria) on 29th June 1964. Once the 1964 summer timetable was over *India* was no longer required at Blackpool and it was drafted north, to 12A Carlisle (Kingmoor), making a final move to 55A Leeds (Holbeck) in May 1965. (H. L. Holland)

9) A fine and sunny 2nd August 1955 heralds the passing of *Coronation* Class 4-6-2 No 46241 *City of Edinburgh*, allocation not known, as it clatters over an exit road leading from the vast and busy marshalling yards at Basford Hall, to the south of Crewe, with a Perth to Euston express. In the left of this picture a freight makes its way out of the yard and heads for the up relief line with a southbound freight. (N. E. Preedy)

10) Class 5 4-6-0 No 45410 and Class 8F 2-8-0 No 48766, both from 2F Bescot shed, near Walsall, steam through Wednesbury, in the West Midlands, passing weed-strewn tracks near to an all but deserted goods depot, with a heavy freight on 14th August 1964. No 45410 ended its days working from 2E Saltley in September 1966, whilst No 48766, based at 5D Stoke, was condemned in February 1967. Both died at the hands of Cashmores, Great Bridge. (T. R. Amos)

11) 'On your bike' has been the maxim of the eighties by certain prominent persons. *Jubilee* Class 4-6-0 No 45650 *Blake* (16A Nottingham) lies at rest in the yard at 14A Cricklewood whilst the employees of the Raleigh bicycle firm enjoy a day out in London. What a pity the powers that be on 31st May 1958 could not have organised No 45639 to be in charge of the outing but there again it was based at Leeds (Holbeck) and not Nottingham. (A. Swain)

12) Long before the electrics came, suburban traffic from Manchester (London Road) — now Piccadilly — to places on the route to Sheffield were worked by LNER C13 Class 4-4-2 Tanks like No 67423. It arrives bunker-first at the terminus on 9th August 1953 with a local passenger train from Glossop. A young spotter adorned in the dress of the day appears to be more interested in the photographer than the engine. (Peter Hay)

13) For many years a regular performer on the West Coast Main Line, *Royal Scot* Class 4-6-0 No 46100 *Royal Scot* was transferred to the Midland Division in November 1959 and allocated to 16A Nottingham. In June 1962 it was transferred to 17A Derby but in August of the same year it returned to Nottingham shed and during the same month was photographed at Nottingham, light engine, two months before withdrawal for preservation. (G. W. Sharpe)

14) A summer breeze wafts surplus steam from right to left outside the running shed on 30th June 1965 from the safety valves of an unidentified Class 5 4-6-0 and a locally based Class 4F 'Duck Six' 0-6-0 No 44294, which is receiving attention at 8B Warrington (Dallam) prior to departing from the depot to take up a freight working. Apart from Dallam there was a small sub-shed at Arpley between Bank Quay and Latchford stations. (Brian Bennett)

15) With a fine array of elevated lower quadrant signals and signalbox providing a superb backcloth Hughes Class 6P5F 'Crab' 2-6-0 No 42849, from 9B Stockport, pilots an unidentified Class 5 4-6-0 into Chester (General) station as they combine to double-head a peak-time Llandudno to Newcastle holiday special (1K20) in August 1963. The former GWR Chester (West) shed is partially visible in the right of this picture. (Kit Windle)

16) Class 5 4-6-0 No 45018, from 12A Carlisle (Kingmoor) deputising for a failed BR *Britannia* Class 4-6-2 nevertheless makes a good ascent of shap, without rear end assistance, with a Warwickshire Railway Society special train on 28th November 1964. The train is seen approaching Greenholme road bridge after a fresh sprinkling of snow had adorned the Fells. No 45018 survived in service at Kingmoor until December 1966. (H. L. Holland)

17) High summer on the Midland in 1958. Class 5 4-6-0 No 45426, a 9A Longsight (Manchester) locomotive, pilots an unident-ified *Jubilee* Class 4-6-0 towards the northern entrance to Seaton Tunnel with a Bradford to St. Pancras express. During the 1960's No 45426 was based at both of the Crewe sheds, Trafford Park, Willesden, Northampton, Banbury, Colwick and Edge Hill (Liverpool) before being withdrawn in March 1968. (A. C. Ingram)

18) *Coronation* Class 4-6-2 No 46231 *Duchess of Atholl*, from 66A Polmadie (Glasgow) storms through Madeley station, on the racing ground from Stafford to Crewe, with the northbound *Royal Scot*, from Euston to Glasgow (Central) on 22nd July 1953. Despite the well maintained platforms, Madeley had closed the previous year and the only intermediate station still open between Stafford and Crewe is at Norton Bridge. (N. E. Preedy)

19) The former Great Central Railway shed at Gorton, in Manchester, was only ten months away from total closure when this picture was taken on 23rd August 1964. Photographed in the shed yard on this day are two 'foreigners', WD Class 8F 2-8-0 No 90706 (8L Aintree) and Class 5 'Caprotti' 4-6-0 No 44741, from 8C Speke Junction, both sheds being in the Liverpool area. Behind No 44741 is another WD Class 8F 2-8-0. (T. R. Amos)

20) Skipton station must have been a draughty place in the winter of 1955, judging by the wagon sheet which the crew of Midland Railway Class 1F 0-6-0T No 41855, a locally based engine, have borrowed in their attempt to keep warm. The sunshine on the massive stone wall behind must herald the forthcoming Spring, which cannot come soon enough even for these hardy Yorkshire railwaymen. (Peter Hay)

21) Despite being nationalised at the beginning of the previous year, the tenders of these locomotives seen in the shed yard at 3D Aston, in Birmingham, still sport the logo's of their previous owner on 13th August 1949. A shed employee, in foreman's or shedmaster's attire, places a lamp on the bracket of Class 5 4-6-0 No 45349. (A. N. H. Glover)

22) Everything looks Great Western — the signals are lower semaphores and the engine is GWR *Hall* Class 4-6-0 No 6906 *Chicheley Hall* but the shedplate tells a different story. The code is 2D once 84C Banbury, now under the auspices of the London Midland Region on 14th June 1964. *Chicheley Hall* heads, tender-first, towards the modernised station, under caution, with a down freight. (Terry Ward)

23) BR Class 5 4-6-0 No 73053, newly transferred to 6D Shrewsbury from 1G Woodford Halse, passes a disused siding with an up express freight on 22nd July 1964, photographed soon after departing from Swan Village station. The lines to the left, opposite the small junction signalbox, lead to Dudley Port and Stourbridge. Swan Village, situated between Wednesbury and West Browich, closed in 1972. (T. R. Amos)

24) Former Midland Railway Class 2P 4-4-0 No 40504, from 16A Nottingham, pilots a BR Class 5 4-6-0 (number unknown) off Harringworth Viaduct, situated between Kettering and Loughborough with a down express — circa 1958. Until rendered redundant by more modern traction the 2P's were a common sight on pilot duties. No 40504 managed to linger on from Nottingham shed until condemned in January 1961. (A. C. Ingram)

25) If one didn't know one's way to steam sheds one landmark to look out for was a gas holder, many of which were located adjacent to depots. Failing this, one could search the horizon for coaling plants similar to the lofty concrete structure at 9K Bolton. Taking on fresh fuel supplies beneath the hopper on 19th June 1967, is Class 8F 2-8-0 No 48646, a visitor from 10D Lostock Hall. (M. S. Stokes)

26) The footplate crew of BR Class 9F 2-10-0 No 92104 take things easy as their charge, from 16G Westhouses, makes light of a four coach local passenger train as it departs from Desborough & Rothwell station on 22nd April 1963. This station, on the line from Kettering to Market Harborough, closed during 1968, living for a year or so longer than No 92104 which succumbed to withdrawal in February 1967. (T. R. Amos)

27) With the North Wales hills in the background, a 6J Holyhead based Class 5 4-6-0 No 45493 skirts the coastline after leaving Penmaenmawr station, between Llanfairfechan and Conway, with a Holyhead to Chester and beyond express, the first two coaches of which are of Gresley vintage, on 20th August 1964. No 45493, which had been a longstanding inmate of 2A Rugby had been drafted to Holyhead in July of the previous year. (T. R. Amos)

28) An especially spruced up former Midland Railway Class 4F 0-6-0 No 43953, 'borrowed' from 12D Workington, darkens the skyline as it blasts out of Clowne, near Langwith, on single track, with an enthusiasts special organised by the Railway Correspondence and Travel Society, on 16th October 1965. Serving no further useful purpose in life, an abandoned loading gauge stands sentinel like over a lifted siding. (T. R. Amos)

29) With its massive bulk dwarfing the leading carriage *Coronation* Class 4-6-2 No 46256 *Sir William A. Stanier F. R. S.* passes Hest Bank station and signalbox and heads homewards towards 1B Camden with an up Glasgow (Central) to Euston express on 1st September 1957. Note the catch-points on the track nearest to the camera. Hest Bank station, situated by Morecambe Bay is now a distant memory on the West Coast Main Line. (R. Butterfield)

30) A double-header in full cry at Clifton on a misty 2nd April 1957. Class 5 4-6-0 No 45332 and BR *Britannia* Class 4-6-2 No 70052 *Firth of Tay*, from sheds as far apart as 10B Preston and 66A Polmadie (Glasgow) respectively, combine to power a Glasgow to Manchester express past the camera. With only a handful of main line diesels in service it is hard to believe that within the next ten years or so both engines would be gone. (R. Butterfield)

31) A severe case of overcrowding at 1E Bletchley engine shed with Unrebuilt *Patriot* Class 4-6-0 No 45546 *Fleetwood*, from 5A Crewe (North) sporting an excursion code of W232 and an unidentified Class 8F 2-8-0 taking up much of the small yard on Wednesday, 7th August 1957. *Fleetwood* was to be withdrawn from 8B Warrington in June 1962 and after a period of storage at Preston shed it was cut up at Crewe Works in August 1962. (J. D. Gomersall)

32) A crisp winter's day highlights the smoke and steam issuing from *Coronation* Class 4-6-2 No 46235 *City of Birmingham*, from the close at hand North shed of 5A, as two young schoolboys, amidst the lengthening shadows on the platform, observe the departure of the same as it accelerates a Holyhead to Euston express out of Crewe in January 1961. There is further steam activity from an unknown engine to the right. (Kit Windle)

33) Ivatt Class 2-6-2T No 41279 at Uppingham, a terminus station, with the stock of a two coach push and pull train to Seaton in the summer of 1958. The passenger service on this branch ceased on 13th June 1960. Although carrying a 15F Market Harborough shedplate No 41279 was actually allocated to 15C Leicester (Midland) being on loan to the former shed. It was withdrawn from Leicester in December 1963. (A. C. Ingram)

34) The partially demolished roof at 14B Kentish Town admits rays of sunshine to enable the photographer to record the presence of MR Class 3F 0-6-0T No 47245, MR Class 4F 0-6-0 No 43964, MR Class 1F 0-6-0T No 41672, Class 4 2-6-4T No 42325 and Class 3 2-6-2T No 40119 as they crowd round the turntable in August 1949. All are local engines and some are still carrying their old numbers in LMS lettering. (G. W. Sharpe)

35 A Class 4P 'Midland Compound' 4-4-0 built for the LMS, No 41185 is respectably clean as it makes off from Flixton towards Manchester (Central) with an 'all stations' local from Liverpool (Central) on 24th August 1952. With the frequent stops along the route it didn't give these engines much chance to show off their speed. No 41185 was taken out of service from 17A Derby in November 1957. (Peter Hay)

36) With a combined tractive effort of 79,340 lbs, steam gushes from the side mounted exhausts of two BR Franco-Crosti Class 9F 2-10-0's Nos 92026 and 92027, both from 15A Wellingborough, as they rattle a train of mineral wagons through Ampthill, south of Bedford, in 1956. In common with the other 'Crosti's', both of these engines reverted at a later date to the more conventional exhaust. (G. W. Sharpe)

37) The warning sign informs us of the overhead electric cables attached to the 'gallows' style supports in this picture — crude but nevertheless deadly. The main subject matter is LNER Thompson B1 Class 4-6-0 No 61130, a visitor to 14D Neasden from 40B Immingham, on 30th April 1962, not many weeks before the closure of the shed. No 61130 is in company with an unidentified BR Class 4 2-6-0. (D. K. Jones)

38) Still bearing the old style BR logo on the tender, a begrimed and rain-soaked 55A Leeds (Holbeck) BR *Britannia* Class 4-6-2 No 70044 *Earl Haig* emerges from beneath a railway overbridge and swings away from the outskirts of Carlisle, near to Upperby shed, with a Glasgow (St. Enoch) to Leeds express during 1959. *Earl Haig* had been at 9A Longsight (Manchester) until its transfer to Holbeck in November 1958. (G. W. Sharpe)

39) A 'room with a view' is something we all like but to have one with a view of a railway line during steam days is another thing. The camera looks down upon two rows of houses, all with neatly kept gardens and two (by now) collectors items — cars, as Class 5 4-6-0 No 45430 (21D Aston) emerges from behind the rooftops and takes the Aston line at Stechford with a freight train on 26th June 1960. (Mike Wood)

40) The fireman takes a breather as his charge Class 8F 2-8-0 No 48185, from 18A Toton, passes the 'Majorca Club' and trundles past the camera at Stapleford & Sandiacre station, closed in 1967, with a lengthy and heavily loaded coal train on 17th May 1962. Some of the wagons are constructed of wood, what a great fire risk combination — coal and wood — whilst the majority are built of metal. (B. W. L. Brooksbank)

41) Two former Midland Railway workhorses Class 3F 0-6-0's Nos 43449 and 43565 drift past Bedford (Midland) station, light engine, prior to returning to their home shed, coded 14E, in January 1960. Despite their unkempt external condition both engines survived at Bedford until 1962, with 43565 being condemned in June and No 43449 three months later. Both were scrapped at Derby Works. (T. Hailes)

42) The former Lancashire & Yorkshire shed — 24A Accrington —was one of the first major sheds on the London Midland Region to close to steam. Its demise came on 6th March 1961 when it was used to house and service diesel multiple units. Photographed in the shed yard on a gloomy day in the mid-fifties are two WD Class 8F 2-8-0's, one being identified as No 90112, native to Accrington. (R. Butterfield)

43) A small boy, his spotting book clasped firmly in his left hand, waves to the footplate crew of a filthy Ivatt Class 4 2-6-0 No 43045, from a rain-soaked platform at Lancaster (Green Ayre) station as the engine travels light engine on Monday, 22nd February 1965. No 43045 is a visitor to Green Ayre from 10A Carnforth. On the left a lone railwayman makes his way on foot to the nearby steam shed, coded 10J. (A. C. Ingram)

44) A few deft touches of white paint can make all the difference to a steam engine especially when its outward appearance has already been smartened up. Hughes Class 6P5F 2-6-0 No 42727, newly transferred to 8H Birkenhead from 9B Stockport, is being employed on a Stephenson Locomotive Society special from Birmingham on 27th March 1966, being photographed at Mold Junction on the outskirts of Chester. (N. E. Preedy)

45) The Drummond & McIntosh Class 0F 0-4-0 Saddle Tanks were introduced in 1885 by the Caledonian Railway and although the bulk of their ranks were allocated to sheds in Scotland, over the years a few found employment as shunters at Crewe Works because of their short wheelbase. On 26th February 1950 No 56032 simmers between duties at Crewe. It remained in service at Crewe until withdrawn in October 1960. (A. N. H. Glover)

46) Two ex. Great Central Railway O4 Class 2-8-0's at rest, in tandem, in the shed yard at 6F Bidston, Wirral in the summer of 1961. At the forefront is O4/3 No 63713, from 9G Gorton, a type fitted with a steam brake only and no water scoop. These locomotives were employed on the Bidston to Shotton iron ore trains. Note the dilapidated structure behind the engines. (Kit Windle)

47) *Coronation* Class 4-6-2 No 46254 *City of Stoke-on-Trent*, from 5A Crewe (North) keeps well away from the electrified track as it coasts through Carpenders Park as it nears the end of its journey with a Liverpool (Lime Street) to Euston express on 1st August 1962. *City of Stoke-on-Trent*, constructed at Crewe Works in 1946, one of the non-streamlined series was withdrawn in October 1964. (John Stones)

48) In common with the Midlands much of the former GWR system in mid-Wales including a large section of the coastal railway was taken over by the London Midland authorities in 1962/63. On 13th July 1964 the fireman of 6F Machynlleth based BR Class 4 4-6-0 No 75004 prepares to hand over the single line token to the signalman at Criccieth station as it arrives with the 1.38 pm Dovey Junction to Pwllheli passenger. (R. Picton)

49) Under the watchful gaze of the occupant of the signalbox, WD Class 8F 2-8-0 No 90313, based at 41D Canklow, passes through Loughborough (Midland) station on the Midland main line with a northbound Class 8 iron-ore freight on 11th April 1964. This may well have been one of the last duties performed by No 90313 as it was condemned this same month. It was cut up at Smith's, Ecclesfield in July 1964. (K. L. Seal)

50) Class 3F 'Jinty' 0-6-0T No 47341 takes a break between duties in the yard of its home shed at 9A Longsight (Manchester) on 18th September 1959. Due to the early electrification of the main line from Crewe to Manchester (Piccadilly) the bulk of Longsight's premier passenger power was transferred away by the end of 1960, leaving engines of more secondary importance at the depot. (D. K. Jones)

51) An unidentified ex. Midland Railway Class 3F 0-6-0 hustles along at Bennerley Junction, Ilkeston with a load of mineral empties bound for the collieries on 17th April 1959. By this date the traditional wooden coal wagon was being rapidly replaced by the more modern steel variety as seen in the left of this picture. The Class 3F 0-6-0's were rendered extinct by February 1964. (Peter Hay)

52) An almost brand new BR Class 9F 2-10-0 No 92122, from 15A Wellingborough, is a visitor to 18D Staveley (Barrow Hill) on 22nd September 1957. Constructed in March of the same year, No 92122 was to serve from Wellingborough and Leicester (Midland) sheds twice, before moving on to 8H Birkenhead in April 1965. Staveley (Barrow Hill) became the property of the Eastern Region in February 1958. (N. E. Preedy)

53) The feats of Brian Clough and his Nottingham Forest side in recent years have become legendary but the team had its successes long before he arrived on the scene. LNER B1 Class 4-6-0 No 61163 (40E Colwick), complete with an appropriate headboard, is at Neasden Junction on 2nd May 1959, with the stock of a Nottingham-Wembley Stadium Cup Final special. Forest beat Luton 2-1 to lift the F. A. Cup. (B. W. L. Brooksbank)

54) Desolation at Hathern station, between Kegworth and Loughborough, closed in 1960. The empty buildings stand gaunt and derelict and weeds encroach on the partially demolished platforms which are still straddled by a wrought-iron bridge, no longer of any use to would be passengers. Oblivious to it all is, Class 8F 2-8-0 No 48606 (18A Toton) on the Midland main line with a northbound mineral train on 11th May 1963. (K. L. Seal)

55) The former Cheshire Lines Committee station at Mobberley, between Knutsford and Sale, is the setting for this photograph taken on 13th June 1959. Stanier Class 3 2-6-2T No 40094, from 9F Heaton Mersey departs with a local passenger train from Chester. The C. L. C. was formed by a conglomerate from the Great Central, Great Northern and Midland Railways. (N. E. Preedy)

56) Passengers scurry along the platforms in an effort to get out of the chill winter wind and into the comfort of the steam heated carriages of the 12.43 hours (Saturdays Only) Bradford to Morecambe express at Hellifield, on 15th February 1965, which is being hauled by a 10J Lancaster (Green Ayre) Class 5 4-6-0 No 45354. Nine months later and the services of this engine were no longer required by British Railways. (H. L. Holland)

57) 55A Leeds (Holbeck) *Jubilee* Class 4-6-0 No 45661 *Vernon* alongside the shed building at 9B Stockport on 23rd October 1964, after being serviced in readiness for a return working to Leeds. One of the authors had a trip behind *Vernon* from York, with Newcastle-Cardiff express on Saturday, 26th October 1963. Deputising for a diesel failure, *Vernon* itself failed and was replaced by sister engine No 45608 *Gibraltar* at Sheffield. (T. R. Amos)

58) An Unrebuilt *Patriot* Class 4-6-0 No 45511 *Isle of Man*, from 8B Warrington, nears the end of its long career seconded to a more menial task than it was designed for, passing over Brock troughs, between Preston and Garstang, with an up fitted freight on 15th April 1960. *Isle of Man* was transferred to 12B Carlisle (Upperby) in September 1961 but was withdrawn five months later being cut up at Crewe in March 1961. (R. W. Hinton)

59) An overgrown derelict dwelling looks down from the embankment as a work-stained 2E Saltley BR Class 9F 2-10-0 No 92137 sweeps round the curve on the approach to Swan Village station with a Bilston bound iron-ore train on 22nd July 1964. Although under the auspices of the London Midland Region, Swan Village still retained a GWR flavour as these freshly painted signals bear witness to. (T. R. Amos)

60) Having spent many years at sheds in and around the Manchester area, Class 4 2-6-4T No 42287 found itself transferred to the capital, London in April 1965 where it was photographed at its new home, 1A Willesden, in steam in the yard on the second day in the month. No 42287 only lingered at Willesden for three months, moving north once more to 10D Lostock Hall. It ended its days at 56A Wakefield, condemned in July 1967. (D. K. Jones)

61) As if ashamed of itself Class 4F 0-6-0 No 44529 attempts to hide by an overgrown embankment near to the turntable pit at Market Harborough shed on 18th October 1964, a month after being condemned. No 44529 with a sacked chimney was based at 15C Leicester (Midland) but sub-shedded at Market Harborough. It was scrapped a month later at Cohens, Kettering. (T. R. Amos)

62) A panoramic view of the sweeping curve through Wolverton station, some fifty-two miles from Euston. The smoke from Class 5 4-6-0 No 45113 (1F Rugby) momentarily disturbs the overhead wires as it heads north with a down Class 8 freight on 9th April 1964. Wolverton is of course famous for its extensive carriage and wagon works. When first constructed the West Coast Main Line ran through the centre of the works. (K. L. Seal)

63) A former London & North Western Railway Class 7F No 49361, from 2F Bescot, fitted with a tender cab, plods along tender-first at the head of a lengthy loose coupled freight at Wednesbury on 24th July 1964. In January 1957 there were some 207 of these engines in service working from depots on the London Midland and Western Regions. By 1964 there were only three survivors, Nos 48895, 49173 and 49361 and all were gone by the end of the year. (T. R. Amos)

64) A splendid elevated view of the extensive carriage and wagon sidings dissected by the main running lines at Edge Hill, Liverpool on 12th June 1959. *Jubilee* Class 4-6-0 No 45681 *Aboukir*, from the nearby shed 8A, passes empty stock heading for Lime Street station with the 11.05 am express from Liverpool to Euston. In the right of the picture, in the background a Class 3F 0-6-0T fusses around light engine. (B. W. L. Brooksbank)

65) Piles of discarded ash, coal and slack litter the tracks in the shed yard at 5C Stafford in September 1961. The twin towers of the coaling and ash disposal plants, both concrete monoliths, look down upon 84G Shrewsbury Class 5 4-6-0 No 45298, seen paired with a self-weighing tender. Much of the importance of the shed declined as more and more diesel multiple units took over the local passenger workings. (N. E. Preedy)

66) During the early sixties the bulk of expresses on the Midland main line to and from St. Pancras were in the hands of diesel power but on the freight side it was a different story, that is until the mass introduction of Type 2 diesels came along on the Midland Division. On 11th April 1964 Class 8F 2-8-0 No 48376 (15B Wellingborough) lays a trail of smoke to the south of Hathern with an up Class 8 mineral working. (K. L. Seal)

67) The driver of Class 5 4-6-0 No 44811 observes the progress of Class 2P 4-4-0 No 40543 and Class 5 4-6-0 No 45264, both from 15C Leicester (Midland) as they come on shed at 1A Willesden for servicing after working a Corby to Wembley special (M971) on 2nd June 1959. No 44811 may well have arrived with a similar working as it too was allocated to Leicester (Midland). (A. Swain)

68) Maximum track occupation at Acton Bridge station, between Warrington and Crewe in June 1958. An unknown passenger train heading northbound is passed by the up *Royal Scot*, from Glasgow (Central) to Euston on the West Coast Main Line, in the extremely capable hands of *Coronation* Class 4-6-2 No 46245 *City of London* (1B Camden) carrying the appropriate headboard. (N. E. Preedy)

69) Another view of the West Coast Main Line, this time at Farington to the south of Preston. Former Midland Railway Class 4P 'Compound' 4-4-0 No 41193, a 24E Blackpool engine, heads the 4.35 pm Rochdale to Blackpool express towards its destination on 20th June 1957. This train will have joined the WCML at either Standish or Euxton Junctions. No 41193 was withdrawn from 24J Lancaster (Green Ayre) in November 1958. (B. W. L. Brooksbank)

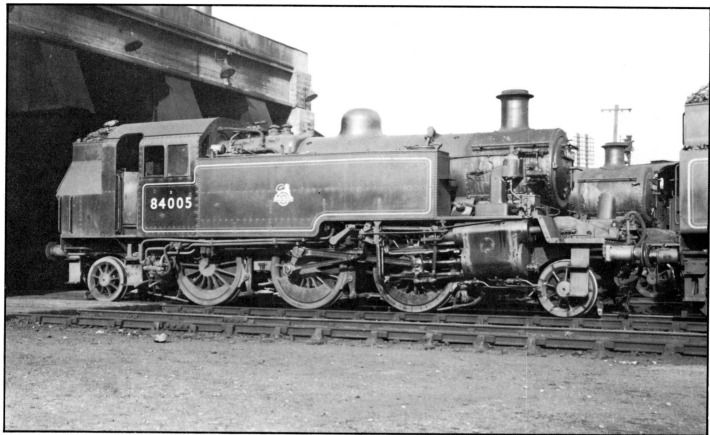

70) A virtually brand new BR Class 2 2-6-2T No 84005 stands outside the running shed of its home base at 15D Bedford on 10th October 1954 in the company of several other tank engines. During its comparatively short working life No 84005 spent all of its days at depots on the Midland Division, being taken out of service in November 1965 from 15A Leicester (Midland). (A. N. H. Glover)

71) The condition of this locomotive is a far cry from the heady days when gleaming GWR *Castles* and *Kings* ruled the roost in the Wolverhampton area. Class 5 4-6-0 No 44684, from 5B Crewe (South) departs from Oxley sidings with a northbound freight on 4th March 1967. Two days later, with the closure of the two remaining sheds in the West Midlands, 2B Oxley and 2E Saltley to steam, steam's association with the area was over. (Mike Wood)

72) Sharp contrasts of sunlight and shadow as Fairburn Class 4 2-6-4T No 42297, a local engine from 10D Lostock Hall, brings the 08.07 hours stopping train from Ormskirk into the East Lancashire side of Preston station on 13th August 1965. Adjacent to No 42297 is BR Class 4 2-6-0 No 75032, a visitor from 8K Bank Hall, Liverpool. The gleaming rails help to add a new dimension to this photograph. (H. L. Holland)

73) 'Thomas The Tank and Friends' gather together in this busy scene at 6G Llandudno Junction on 16th August 1964. Two local Class 3F 0-6-0 Tanks, one of which appears to be tilting over, Nos 47361 and 47507 join forces with Class 5 4-6-0 No 45261 (8A Edge Hill—Liverpool), BR Class 4 4-6-0 No 75017 (8F Springs Branch Wigan) and BR Class 4 4-6-0 No 75048 (8K Bank Hall). (T. R. Amos)

41

74) LMS stalwarts may well wince at the sight of this gleaming Southern Region interloper being included within the pages of an LMR album but in London, due to the vast amount of cross-city lines and transfer yards, engines from other regions often 'trespassed' on rival territory. On a July day in 1958 H16 Class 4-6-2T No 30517 (70B Feltham) departs from Cricklewood with a Brent to Feltham coal train. (A. Swain)

75) Ex. Midland Railway Johnson Class 3F 0-6-0 No 43499, from 15B Kettering, with a Kettering to Oakham pick-up goods approaches Harringworth station, tender-first, in April 1960. Although this station had closed on 1st November 1948 the buildings were still in situ, but nature had reclaimed the platforms. The signalbox, however, was still in service. No 43499 was drafted north to 9G Gorton in June of this same year. (A. C. Ingram)

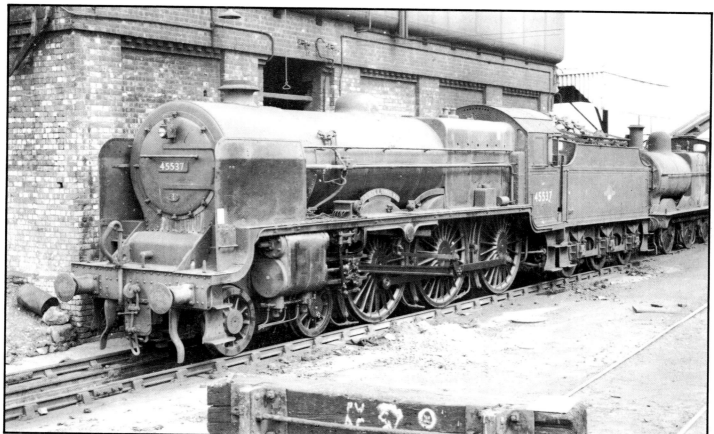

76) 2A Rugby shed plays host to a visitor from the not too far away depot at 2B Nuneaton on an undefined day in 1961. Unre-built *Patriot* Class 4-6-0 No 45537 *Private E. Sykes V.C.* stands out of steam by the water tower in company with an unidentified former M. R. Class 3F 0-6-0. Withdrawn in June 1962, *Private E. Sykes V. C.* was dumped at Rugby shed from April to August 1962 prior to scrapping. (N. E. Preedy)

77) A *Jubilee* Class 4-6-0 No 45705 *Seahorse*, newly allocated to 9D Newton Heath from 10B Blackpool, departs from Leyland with the nine coach 09.47 hours express from Manchester to Blackpool on 29th June 1964. A push-bike leaning against the flimsy fence is a give-away as to the mode of transport used by the photographer to reach this vantage point. (H. L. Holland)

78) A hard at work Class 8F 2-8-0 No 48414, from 16A Toton, belches smoke high into the East Midlands air as it heads a lengthy Class 8 freight towards the camera at Syston, near Leicester in July 1964. No 48414 ended its days at 16B Colwick, on former Eastern Region territory, in October 1966, being put to the torch at Drapers, Hull in February 1967. (D. K. Jones)

79) A long since swept away array of signals oversee the busy lines on the West Coast Main Line at Nuneaton on 1st November 1959. Class 3 2-6-2T No 40207, with a dented side-tank, poses in the shed yard at its home base, coded 2B. Despite being abandoned in November 1957 No 40207 is still sporting the old British Railways emblem. After withdrawal from Nuneaton in February 1962 it was dumped at the disused Coventry shed. (A. N. H. Glover)

80) Photographs emanating from the former LNWR section of the Wolverhampton area appear to be few and far between and so, despite the not perfect quality it was decided to include this print in the album. *Coronation* Class 4-6-2 No 46240 *City of Coventry* (1B Camden), its tender laden with fuel, draws slowly out of the carriage sidings with stock of the 4.20 pm Wolverhampton (High Level) to Euston express on 9th August 1963. (T. R. Amos)

81) With upper and lower semaphores abreast and aft. Class 5 4-6-0 No 45349, a Birmingham based engine from 21D Aston, finds itself employed on a Manchester to Llandudno express in high summer in 1962. It is photographed at another neglected location, from the photographers point of view, Queens Ferry on the North Wales main line, between Chester and Shotton. Queens Ferry station was closed in 1966. (Kit Windle)

82) Years of steam workings have blackened the lofty roof interior of the London terminus at St. Pancras when this photograph was taken in 1959. A railwayman, possibly the guard, is having a word with the footplate crew of Ivatt Class 4 'Flying Pig' 2-6-0 No 43120 (14A Cricklewood), itself in a soot-stained condition, prior to it departing with a down relief express (M798). (M. F. Higson — The Smokebox)

83) *Royal Scot* Class 4-6-0 No 46125 *3rd Carabinier*, another Crewe locomotive, this time from the North shed (5A) takes a drink from the troughs at Dillicar, between Low Gill and Tebay, with an unknown eleven coach express working on 5th April 1957. Both Low Gill and Tebay stations have disappeared into railway history, the first closing in 1960 followed by the latter in 1968. (R. Butterfield)

84) "The Glazier" brake-van railtour of the Locomotive Club of Great Britain visited several freight only lines in the St. Helens area on 25th September 1965, behind Class 3F 'Jinty' 0-6-0T No 47298, from 8G Sutton Oak, (now preserved at Southport). The engine is seen taking water at Ravenhead Junction, the site of divergence from the St. Helens—St. Helens Junction line of the three mile branch to Eccleston. (H. L. Holland)

85) There is a plume of smoke in the far distance as Class 8F 2-8-0 No 48390, a 9F Heaton Mersey engine, approaches the camera on quadrupled track south of Stoneyford Junction, Langley Mill with an up Class F mixed freight on 12th July 1963. For many years, up to March 1961 No 48390 was based at 17A Derby. It moved across Manchester to 9H Patricroft in January 1966 being withdrawn from there in May 1968. (B. W. L. Brooksbank)

86) Sheep graze unconcerned on the grasslands whilst the mist hangs over the hills in the background as a 55A Leeds (Holbeck) *Jubilee* Class 4-6-0 No 45593 *Kolhapur* traverses Ribblehead Viaduct on the Settle & Carlisle main line with an express working during 1967. Withdrawn in October 1967, *Kolhapur* has been preserved for posterity at Tyseley. Note the black and white markings on the signal post, helping identification. (Mike Turner)

87) Class 4F 0-6-0 No 44554 is surrounded by Class 8F 2-8-0's outside its home shed at 15E Coalville on 26th February 1964. There are some sister 0-6-0's parked alongside the depot. No 44554, minus shedplate, had arrived at Coalville from 9F Heaton Mersey during the same month but only lasted there for a few months, being condemned in August 1964. Scrapping came at Cashmores, Great Bridge in January 1965. (N. E. Preedy)

88) The tall chimney of a gaunt mill along with various other premises, including some 'Coronation Street' style dwellings form a backcloth as Class 5 4-6-0 No 44930, a 24E Blackpool engine, enters Kirkham & Wesham station, between Blackpool and Preston with the 12.50 pm local passenger from Blackpool (Central) to Manchester (Victoria) on 8th September 1962. No 44930 is hauling a motley set of coaching stock. (B. W. L. Brooksbank)

89) An enthusiast takes advantage of the warm sunshine whilst he savours the smells that only a steam engine can produce from the open window of an express departing from Manchester (Victoria) in the summer of 1967, being hauled by Class 5 4-6-0 No 45287, from 8A Edge Hill (Liverpool). In the twilight of its career No 45287 was to serve from two more depots, 9H Patricroft and 10F Rose Grove before withdrawal in August 1968. (Christopher Fifield)

90) A senior member of the spotting fraternity bows his head and takes notes as another, looking like a fugitive, scuttles across tracks which enter the erecting shop at Crewe Works on 2nd August 1962. After repairs, *Jubilee* Class 4-6-0 No 45700 *Amethyst* awaits the final touches and to be re-united with its tender before being despatched to its home shed at 26A Newton Heath. (D. K. Jones)

91) With the contents of the trucks possibly already devoured, Class 8F 2-8-0 No 48201 (16E Kirkby) leaves Repton & Willington power station, just south of Derby, with an empty coal train on 16th August 1966. No 48201 was despatched to 9B Stockport three months later, making a final move to 9F Heaton Mersey in October 1967 before being made redundant in March 1968. (K. L. Seal)

92) Under clear signals and sporting the mysterious reporting number of 9T43 on its smokebox, Class 5 4-6-0 No 44770, a 6J Holyhead locomotive, speeds light engine, tender-first, past the camera towards a small signalbox at Colwyn Bay in June 1965. Transferred to 5D Stoke in December 1966, No 44770 was condemned from 12A Carlisle (Kingmoor) in October 1967 and scrapped at McWilliams, Shettleston. (N. L. Browne)

93) For many years at 16B Kirkby, Class 4F 0-6-0 No 44118 found itself allocated to 16C Derby on 24th June 1964 where it was being employed on a freight turn at Derby station. Note the sliding top tender. The signalbox in the background controls the entrance and exit roads to the engine sidings. The double dummy and twin lower quadrant signals help to complete the picture. (B. W. L. Brooksbank)

94) A mixture of colour and semaphore signals at Preston on 17th August 1963. BR Class 4 4-6-0 No 75046, from 27A Bank Hall, drifts under a smoke-blackened road bridge and enters the station, overlooked by grey, drab buildings, with the 1.35 pm combined Fleetwood/Blackpool (North) to Manchester (Victoria) stopping train. No 75046 ceased its long association with Bank Hall shed in April 1966 when it moved to 9F Heaton Mersey. (B. W. L. Brooksbank)

95) A packed house at 8F Springs Branch Wigan on 11th May 1964. Included in the line-up in the shed yard are BR Class 4 4-6-0 No 75042, Class 8F 2-8-0 No 48176 and Class 4 2-6-4T No 42631. Nos 42631 and 75042 are Springs Branch engines but No 48176 is a visitor from 8A Edge Hill (Liverpool). No 42631 was withdrawn later in the year but the other two were to survive for a further three years. (D. K. Jones)

96) With their arms raised aloft like a guard of honour outside a church these upper semaphores signal a busy time at Salwick, between Kirkham and Preston on 1st August 1959. Hughes Class 6P5F 'Crab' 2-6-0 No 42844 (24F Fleetwood) races through the station in an attempt to keep ahead of the express looming in the distance. No 42844 is in charge of the 10.20 am Fleetwood-Manchester (Victoria) train. (B. W. L. Brooksbank)

97) With the driver seated comfortably WD Class 8F 2-8-0 No 90674, from 40E Colwick, on the outskirts of Nottingham, clanks through Northampton (Spencer Bridge) with a freight working on 1st July 1963. Despite the shoddy external condition of No 90674 it was to soldier on at Colwick until condemned in August 1965. It was then reduced to scrap by the firm of Arnott Young at Parkgate & Rawmarsh. (Terry Ward)

98) LMS and BR locomotives congregate around the shed yard and concrete coaling plant at 5D Stoke on 23rd August 1964. Nearest the camera is Class 5 4-6-0 No 45387 whilst to the right facing us is BR Class 4 4-6-0 No 75053. Both are Stoke engines. The main running shed is behind the batch of engines including No 75053. Stoke also possessed a small roundhouse, out of sight to the right. (T. R. Amos)

99) Scaffolding and temporary boarding at Euston whilst the station was being rebuilt on 28th May 1963. Passengers make their way to the exit after arriving on a relief express from Liverpool (Lime Street) behind a shy 8A Edge Hill (Liverpool) 'Black 5' 4-6-0 No 45015 hiding behind a tilted 1Z16 reporting number. Note the crude but potentially deadly 'buffer-stop'. (A. F. Nisbet)

100) A six coach local passenger train from St. Helens arrives at Glazebrook, to the west of Manchester on 11th August 1953. Unsuitable motive power is provided by former Great Central Railway 'Director' D10 Class 4-4-0 No 62658 *Prince George*, allocation not known. This is a rare photograph of one of these locomotives. There were a total of ten members of the class which were rendered extinct during the fifties. (Peter Hay)

101) Almost at the end of its working life, BR *Britannia* Class 4-6-2 No 70012 *John of Gaunt* (12A Carlisle—Kingmoor), bereft of all identifying plates, passes Greenholme, Shap with an up goods on 26th August 1967. During its short career *John of Gaunt* worked from 30A Stratford, 32A Norwich, 32D Yarmouth South Town, 31B March, 1A Willesden, 5A Crewe (North), 5B Crewe (South), 6G Llandudno Junction and Kingmoor sheds. (N. E. Preedy)

102) One of the (then) new block trains, carrying cars from the British Motor Corporation at Longbridge, Birmingham to Scotland, passes through Coppull, closed in 1969, at the end of the seventeen mile climb from Warrington behind a filthy Class 5 4-6-0 No 45131, from 8C Speke Junction, on 14th November 1964. By the end of the journey the gleaming cars would no doubt have a covering of soot and cinders. (H. L. Holland)

103) With a good head of steam to spare Class 4F 0-6-0 No 44262, a 17D Rowsley 'Duck Six', heads for Dove Holes Tunnel with a winding freight train on 30th March 1957. No 44262 is paired with a sliding top tender for Peak District working. It was withdrawn from Rowsley shed, later recoded 17C and then 16J, in September 1963. The shed became a sub of Derby in May 1964 and closed completely in March 1967. (R. W. Hinton)

104) Two local residents stand in front of the four road running shed at 6G Llandudno Junction on 20th May 1962. *Royal Scot* Class 4-6-0 No 46144 *Honourable Artillery Company* is alongside Class 5 'Caprotti' 4-6-0 No 44740. Behind No 44740 is a sister engine. *Honourable Artillery Company* moved on to 5A Crewe (North) in June 1963 but No 44740 was condemned from Llandudno Junction in April 1963. (D. Harrison)

105) Having passed the lofty Warrington South signalbox, Class 5 4-6-0's Nos 44802 and 45441, both from 6J Holyhead, double-head the 4.30 pm Manchester (Exchange) to Llandudno express into Warrington (Bank Quay) station on 8th September 1962. Within a matter of weeks both engines had been transferred away from Holyhead, No 44802 to 12A Carlisle (Kingmoor) and No 45441 to 8C Speke Junction. (B. W. L. Brooksbank)

106) A dull scene at Salford is brightened up by the arrival of BR Class 4 4-6-0 No 75015, a 27C Southport based engine, with empty coaching stock from Bolton on 9th June 1959. An array of short, stumpy signals peer above the squat signalbox which is guarded by two 'sentry boxes' belonging to the permanent way department. (B. W. L. Brooksbank)

107) This LMS Class 2P 4-4-0 running into Derby on 25th August 1952, in the new BR lined livery, represents the locomotive outline of the Midland Railway in its last years. No 40359 (18C Hasland) was theoretically a rebuild of one of Johnson's graceful and curvy beauties, but in fact the tender was about all that remained of the older engine. The leading carriages are Stanier pattern LMS, in their new livery of red and cream. (Peter Hay)

108) A bedraggled locally based former Midland Railway Class 3F 0-6-0 No 43585 (24H) shunts coaching stock through the rain at Hellifield on 8th June 1959. The depot at Hellifield can just be made out over the tops of the carriages. No 43585 was condemned from the depot in September 1962 and cut up at Horwich Works. Next to No 43585 there is a painting advertising the London Midland Region. (B. W. L. Brooksbank)

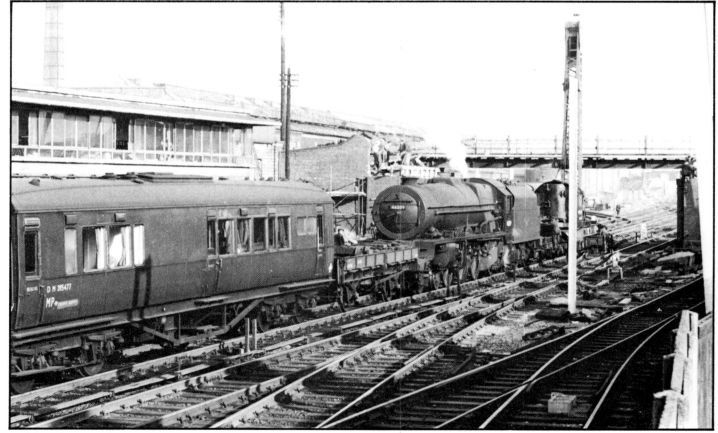

109) Who would have thought in years gone by that a Stanier Pacific would be reduced in status by being employed on an engineers train but these were desperate times for the *Princess* Class 4-6-2's, grateful for any kind of employment. No 46209 *Princess Beatrice*, from 5A Crewe (North), simmers by Stafford North signalbox — circa 1961, whilst modernisation is carried out around it. (G. W. Sharpe)

110) The gloomy confines of Manchester (London Road) overlooks *Royal Scot* Class 4-6-0 No 46161 *King's Own*, from 1B Camden, after the end of its journey from London (Euston) with the down *Comet* in 1955. Various hoardings advertise this, that and the other, along with explicit instructions of how to find one's way to the Station Masters Office, also the parcels office, cloak room and telegraph office. (D. K. Jones)

111) Strange bedfellows at Horwich Works on 21st September 1963 where 9B Stockport *Jubilee* Class 4-6-0 No 45596 *Bahamas* (equipped with a double chimney) is sandwiched between a guards van and a 'Lowmac' wagon shortly after arriving for repairs. The tender from *Bahamas* is loaded onto the 'Lowmac' (for reasons unknown). No 45596 emerged again from the works, lasting until July 1966 and is today preserved. (H. L. Holland)

112) The masts are erected but as yet there are no wires, at Ashton, near Roade, between Wolverton and Rugby (Midland), on 16th September 1963. Relegated to a more menial duty by diesel power *Royal Scot* Class 4-6-0 No 46156 *The South Wales Borderer*, from 1A Willesden, powers an up northbound express past the camera. *The South Wales Borderer* was further demoted when it was transferred to 16B Annesley in November 1962. (Terry Ward)

113) Although once owned by the North British Railway and the Scottish Region of British Railways, Carlisle (Canal) became the property of the London Midland Region in February 1958 and remained so until the depot closed in 1963. Many of the residents were of LNER and NBR origins, including N15 Class 0-6-2T No 69155, photographed in the shed yard on 3rd April 1961. It was withdrawn in September 1962. (A. N. H. Glover)

114) Class 8F 2-8-0 No 48518, a 1A Willesden locomotive, passes the disused platforms and the still in service Hathern Station signalbox, with a southbound Class 8 loose-coupled freight train on 11th April 1964. To the left all of the tracks which once adorned the goods yard have been lifted, with only some surplus sleepers and fishplates remaining to bear witness that there had been lines there. (K. L. Seal)

115) Part of the overall roof straddling two platforms had been removed at Rochdale where Hughes Class 6P5F 'Crab' 2-6-0 No 42724 (26B Agecroft) is captured by the camera with the 11.58 am Wakefield (Kirkgate) to Manchester (Victoria) local passenger on 10th June 1959. In the bay platform to the right of No 42724, is Stanier Class 4 2-6-4T No 42653 (26C Bolton) with another local, bound for Bolton. (B. W. L. Brooksbank)

116) BR *Clan* Class 4-6-2 No 72004 *Clan MacDonald*, shedded at 66A Polmadie (Glasgow), pauses on wet, slippery rails at Penrith, on a rain-drenched day in August 1957, with an up express working. *Clan MacDonald*, constructed in 1952, enjoyed a brief spell at 64A St. Margarets (Edinburgh) from November 1959 to March 1960, before returning to Polmadie where it was to die in December 1962. Darlington claimed the remains. (T. Wright)

117) The fireman of begrimed Class 8F 2-8-0 No 48765, from 41E Staveley (Barrow Hill), relaxes as his mount steams through Stoneyford Junction, Langley Hill, with an up Class 8 freight on 12th July 1963. When the Eastern Region took over control of the former LMR sheds at Canklow, Grimesthorpe and Barrow Hill in February 1958 a number of these 8F's remained on their books. No 48765 was drafted to the LMR in May 1964. (B. W. L. Brooksbank)

118) Spotters throng to the left of this photograph during an 'Open Day' at Crewe Works on 8th April 1962. Two *Royal Scot* Class 4-6-0's Nos 46132 *The King's Regiment Liverpool* (21A Saltley) — partially painted and 46145 *The Duke of Wellington's Regt. (West Riding)*, from 56D Mirfield, fresh from repair, wait to be reunited with their tenders by the traverser near to the erecting shops. (F. Hornby)

119) Its days of glory all but over, *Royal Scot* Class 4-6-0 No 46140 *The King's Royal Rifle Corps*, newly allocated to 9A Long-sight (Manchester) but minus shedplate, leans to a curve at Llandudno Junction station on 24th July 1963, while working the 9.20 am Crewe to Holyhead express. *The King's Royal Rifle Corps* was transferred to 12A Carlisle (Kingmoor) in October 1964, becoming one of the last active members of the class. (H. L. Holland)

120) A gloomy day in June 1967 brings an air of impending doom to the depot with closure on the immediate horizon. During the mid-sixties, as shed after shed demised, surviving steam locomotives were shunted around the remaining depots, until they too succumbed. Thus is the case with BR Class 4 4-6-0 No 75047 newly transferred to 5D Stoke after the closure of 6C Croes Newydd to steam. No 75047 only lived on for a further two months. (Mike Turner)

121) Class 5 4-6-0 No 45351, from 12A, later 12B Carlisle (Upperby), sweeps beneath catenary masts as it arrives at Lancaster station with a Barrow to Euston express on a misty 3rd April 1957. This engine was transferred briefly to 24K Preston in June 1960, returning to Upperby the following month. It later served at 12A Carlisle (Kingmoor), 9K Bolton and 10D Lostock Hall, before being condemned in August 1965. (R. Butterfield)

122) The LNER J11 Class 0-6-0's or 'Pom-Pom's' were the successors to the J10's and a significant advance in power. A goods engine with a shine like the one on No 64435 was a rarity, photographed on 26th August 1952, but this loco seems aware of someone's care for it and is making good speed with a loose-coupled freight heading westwards on the CLC near to Chassen Road, between Flixton and Urmston. (Peter Hay)

123) 'Flying Pig', Ivatt Class 4 2-6-0 No 43042, a 15B Kettering inmate, passes milepost 84, mid-way between Gretton and Harringworth stations, with the 8.20 am 'Manton pick-up' freight from Kettering to Oakham — circa 1958. Note the reporting number 31 on the lamp-iron. No 43042 was re-allocated to 9F Heaton Mersey in September 1962 and worked from there until no longer required in February 1966. (A. C. Ingram)

124) Whilst on the subject of Heaton Mersey shed we switch our attentions to the very same with this excellent interior shot, as taken in March 1968. The main subject matter is focussed on Class 8F 2-8-0 No 48471, a recent transfer to the depot from 9L Buxton. The untidy pipe-work on the loco's boiler is a give-away to the fact that the engine had once been based on the Western Region and had been 'Swindonised'. (M. S. Stokes)

125) High summer on the West Coast Main Line and one can almost hear the singing of a hovering skylark over the field. Lofty signals and tall chimneys dominate the background as BR *Britannia* Class 4-6-2 No 70052 *Firth of Tay*, from 5A Crewe (North), heads the down *Lakes Express* (the 10.30 am from Euston), with portions for Carlisle, Barrow and Windermere, past clear signals on the approach to Preston on 29th June 1964. (H. L. Holland)

126) Permanent way workers stand aside as an unkempt 15C Leicester (Midland) *Jubilee* Class 4-6-0 No 45585 *Hyderabad* steams through Chinley on 4th April 1960 with the St. Pancras bound up *Palatine*. *Hyderabad*, one of a batch of *Jubilee's* which carried names from the various states in India, spent much of its working life on former Midland Railway metals; being taken out of service from 16C Derby in May 1964. (N. E. Preedy)

127) Under the watchful gaze of the signalman entombed in the warm confines of Brickyard Crossing box, ex. MR Class 4F 0-6-0 No 43979 (2E Saltley) trundles a freight towards St. Andrews Junction, on the Camp Hill avoiding line, with Class 4F 0-6-0 No 44211, also from Saltley, lending rear end assistance on 22nd February 1964. There is no evidence today of either the signalbox or the crossing. (P. A. Rowlings)

128) The small sub-shed and yard at Market Harborough on 23rd June 1963 is occupied by Class 4F 0-6-0 No 44414 (15C Leicester-Midland), Class 8F 2-8-0 No 48082 (15B Kattering), Stanier Class 6P5F 2-6-0 No 42950 (2B Nuneaton) and Ivatt Class 2 2-6-2T No 41279, another Leicester (Midland) engine. These were withdrawn from service in May 1965, April 1967, November 1965 and December 1963 respectively. (T. R. Amos)

129) Having shunted and assembled a freight train in the goods yard at Southport on 11th August 1964, Ivatt Class 2 2-6-2T No 41217 departs in a flurry of steam for local stations in the area. The shed to which No 41217 belongs (8M) is in the background and has since been saved for posterity by the preservationists, after closure in June 1966. No 41217 was condemned from 12A Carlisle (Kingmoor) in December 1966. (H. L. Holland)

130) To all intensive purposes this locomotive outline is that of a *Royal Scot* but on closer inspection we find that it is indeed one of the two rebuilt *Jubilee's*, No 45736 *Phoenix*, from 5A Crewe (North), being employed on a short five coach express at Hest Bank on 20th May 1956. *Phoenix* had been rebuilt in 1942, having its power classification increased from 6P5F to 7P, along with No 45735 *Comet*. (R. Butterfield)

131) Enjoying the warm summer sunshine the driver of Class 4F 0-6-0 No 44389, a 6G Llandudno engine, looks back to check that all is well as he eases an up freight out of the yard at Penmaenmawr on 25th July 1963 and heads for the North Wales main line. This engine was a particular favourite at Llandudno shed having been there for many years but they parted company when it was sent to 10G Skipton in December 1964. (H. L. Holland)

132) The ugly signs of modernisation, the overhead electrification masts and concrete flyover at Bletchley, are partially nullified by the presence of *Jubilee* Class 4-6-0 No 45733 *Novelty*, from 1A Willesden, seen arriving at the station with a Euston to Northampton local stopping train on 3rd August 1964. *Novelty* found itself transferred to 5A Crewe (North) the following month but was withdrawn almost straight away. (C. P. Stacey)

133) When the time came for an overhaul, 5B Crewe (South's) 'Jinty' Class 3F 0-6-0T No 47482 was strangely despatched to Darlington Works, rather than the close at hand local plant. When it returned Darlington had applied the side numbers to the water tanks, rather than the cabs. It is seen here on station pilot duties at Crewe station on 19th September 1964, in company with English Electric Type 4 No D376. (W. Potter)

134) An unidentified 0-6-0 diesel shunter dwarfs a former Lancashire & Yorkshire Class OF 0-4-0ST No 51237, in the yard of its home shed at 26B Agecroft during 1961. Also 'towering' above this little engine is Class 3F 'Jinty' 0-6-0T No 47579, another of Agecroft's inmates. No 51237 had been transferred to this shed from 27A Bank Hall in December 1960 but No 47579 had been here for many years. (B. J. Miller)

135) Although rostered steam had finished at 2A Tyseley on 7th November 1966, locomotives came to the shed from far and wide for wheel turning. Dumped unceremoniously beneath two loading guages outside a roundhouse on 7th May 1967, is BR *Britannia* Class 4-6-2 No 70049 *Solway Firth* (with stencilled names on the deflectors), from 12A Carlisle (Kingmoor), a shed it was to die at in December of the same year. (Mike Wood)

136) Steam streams upwards from the safety valves of Class 4F 0-6-0 No 44543, a 26A Newton Heath locomotive, as it awaits its next banking duty up the Miles Platting incline at Manchester (Victoria) on 9th June 1959. No 44543, a longstanding resident at Newton Heath and paired with a tender-cab, was eventually withdrawn from there in May 1964 and scrapped at the Slag Reduction Company, Rotherham. (B. W. L. Brooksbank)

137) Class 8F 2-8-0 No 48688 (1E Bletchley) enters Castlethorpe station on the West Coast Main Line, between Roade and Wolverton, with a train being used to remove dismantled track from just north of the station, on 30th August 1964. The reporting number 13N perched on the smokebox of No 48688 may well point to the fact that more than one of these trains were at work under the non-energised wires. (K. L. Seal)

138) Fairburn Class 4 2-6-4T No 42686, from 14C St. Albans, traverses the track approaching St. Albans City station with a six coach St. Pancras to St. Albans local on 30th August 1958. Soon the encroaching ranks of diesel multiple units would sweep steam from these local services, causing the shed at St. Albans to fall victim to modernisation, ridding itself of its allocation of steam power by February 1960. (B. W. L. Brooksbank)

139) A fine panoramic view of the patchwork of fields which epitomize the English landscape, as taken from the heights above Seaton tunnel in 1960. Stanier Class 8F 2-8-0 No 48609, from 15B Kettering, is set to plunge into the darkness of the tunnel with a freight train mainly consisting of stone hoppers. No 48609 ended its days at 9H Patricroft, being taken out of revenue earning service in January 1968. (A. C. Ingram)

140) It was not often that one could see two engines in numerical sequence together on shed, let alone, side by side. Whether by coincidence or arrangement, two 20A Leeds (Holbeck) Class 5 'Caprotti' 4-6-0's find themselves stabled together around an open turntable at 17A Derby on 21st February 1954. Nos 44755 and 44756 also had numerical stablemates at Holbeck, Nos 44753/54/57 but all were drafted away by November 1963. (A. N. H. Glover)

141) A trio of Stanier locomotives in steam in the shed yard at 9D Newton Heath in 1967 all ready for their next tasks. Two are unidentified Class 8F 2-8-0's whilst the third is Class 5 4-6-0 No 45203 which had been allocated to Newton Heath for many a year along with another numerical coincidence, No 45202. Even after both had been withdrawn from 9D in June 1968, they could not be parted until cut up at Drapers, Hull. (Christopher Fifield)

142) With brooding hills in the background Class 5 4-6-0 No 44844, from 5B Crewe (South), labours past the remote 'Summit' signalbox at Ais Gill, on the Settle & Carlisle main line, with a down freight on 25th August 1966. To the right of No 44844 is an unidentified Ivatt Class 4 2-6-0 on an engineers train which had been shunted in the loop. (Alan Bailey)

143) Fowler Class 4 2-6-4T No 42352, based at 15C Leicester (Midland) scuttles over the crude crossing at Broughton Abbey station as it arrives with a Rugby (Midland) to Leicester (London Road) local passenger train on 24th April 1961. These services were withdrawn during 1962 and Broughton Abbey was closed as were the surviving intermediate stations at Ullesthorpe, Leire Halt, Countesthorpe and Wigston South. (B. W. L. Brooksbank)

144) An immaculate Scottish based *Coronation* Class 4-6-2 No 46222 *Queen Mary*, from 66A Polmadie (Glasgow), sizzles in the shed yard at 12A Carlisle (Kingmoor) on 3rd April 1961. Records show that *Queen Mary* emerged from Crewe Works after overhaul in late July 1962, but within less than a month she was stored at her home shed. However, 46222 was returned to service and survived until October 1963. (A. N. H. Glover)

145) By 1964 parts of the former Western Region territory were well and truly in the clutches of the London Midland Region. BR Class 3 2-6-2T No 82003, from 6F Machynlleth, still carries the old style BR logo as it waits patiently at Portmadoc station for the arrival of BR Class 4 4-6-0 No 75004, another Machynlleth locomotive, on 13th July 1964. Both engines are on local passenger workings. (R. Picton)

146) Sunday night was lighting up time in loco sheds all over the country as engines were prepared for work on Monday morning. Ex. Lancashire & Yorkshire Class 3F 0-6-0 No 52461, with a full tender of coal and a lazy pall of smoke from the chimney, had just been lit up inside the running shed at 26C Bolton on Sunday, 27th May 1956. In company with No 52461 is Class 3 2-6-2T No 40133. (J. D. Gomersall)

147) 15A Wellingborough BR Class 9F 2-10-0 No 92126 lifts its safety valves at Harpenden, on the former Midland Railway main line between Luton and St. Albans, with an up London bound freight on 29th August 1957. Harpenden used to have two stations — Central (MR) and East (GN) but the latter closed during 1965. (N. E. Preedy)

148) Having just crossed the River Mersey at Moore Stanier *Coronation* Class 4-6-2 No 46247 *City of Liverpool*, from 1B Camden, heads towards Warrington with a Glasgow (Central) to Euston express on 18th August 1957. The lines to the right of *City of Liverpool* lead from Manchester (London Road) to Chester and beyond. No 46247 was one of a number of *Coronation's* painted in maroon livery. (N. E. Preedy)

149) An Ivatt Class 4 'Flying Pig' flies by the camera, light engine, at Willesden, near to its home shed, on 13th August 1965, a month before it was transferred to its final base at 5D Stoke, being condemned from there in November 1966. During the latters years of its life No 43018 was also shedded at 15C Leicester (Midland), 24J Lancaster (Green Ayre), 12D Kirkby Stephen, 12A Carlisle (Kingmoor) and 1C Watford. (D. K. Jones)

150) A chilly early Spring day is brightened up by the appearance of Class 8F 2-8-0 No 48089, a 9F Heaton Mersey engine, south of Kegworth on the Midland main line, with a southbound freight train on 6th April 1964. Kegworth station, situated between Trent and Loughborough, closed during 1968, two years after No 48089 was withdrawn from Heaton Mersey shed in February 1966. (K. L. Seal)

151) Another view of the vast railway scene at Edge Hill (Liverpool), this time looking away from Lime Street, as photographed on 12th June 1959. With steam to spare *Jubilee* Class 4-6-0 No 45703 *Thunderer*, from 5A Crewe (North) heads the 9.15 am Birmingham (New Street) to Liverpool (Lime Street) express. Judging by the fact that the tender is well filled, *Thunderer* may well have been put in charge of the train at Crewe. (B. W. L. Brooksbank)

152) An LNWR 'Super D' Class 7F 0-8-0 No 49402, allocation not known, awaits attention in the yard at Crewe Works on 26th February 1950, where it may well have lost its LMS logo when it was returned to traffic. No 49402, in company with an unidentified Unrebuilt *Royal Scot* Class 4-6-0, spent its latter years based at 8F Springs Branch Wigan, being condemned from there in November 1962. (A. N. H. Glover)

153) A tender-first 8F Springs Branch Wigan Class 5 4-6-0 No 44814 steams under the wires near to Rugby (Midland) with a lengthy mixed freight on 20th May 1964. No 44814 had been allocated to 21A Saltley for many years before moving to Springs Branch in April 1964 and served from 1G Woodford Halse, 6J Holyhead, 6D Shrewsbury and 5B Crewe (South) before begin rendered redundant in September 1967. (D. K. Jones)

154) Once based at 67D Ardrossan, in Scotland, Fairburn Class 4 2-6-4T No 42210 had been drafted south of the border in February 1960, to 6C Birknhead. By June 1964 it found itself allocated to 12E Tebay where it was to spend the remainder of its life on banking duties. On 28th November 1964, No 42210 drifts down from Shap summit and passes under Greenholme road bridge on its way back to Tebay to await the next duty. (H. L. Holland)

155) Displaying a somewhat charred smokebox, Class 3F 'Jinty' 0-6-0T stands in the yard of its home shed at 8C Speke Junction in the summer of 1960. Peeping from behind No 47388 is Class 5 4-6-0 No 45106, a visitor to the shed from 12B Carlisle (Upperby). Speke Junction used to be the subject of the classic line — "How do you get your budgie to Speke (speak)?" — "Board the 82 bus in the city centre." (D. K. Jones)

156) A mass of overhead wires and masts makes the railway scene at Bletchley look extremely untidy as the winter sun reflects off a locally based Class 3F 'Jinty' 0-6-0T No 47307 as it sets back from the up fast line into the station on 10th December 1964. Apart from the engine other links from the past still remained, signalling wires and point rodding, along with the active signalbox in the right background. (H. L. Holland)

157) With distant spires in the background Class 8F 2-8-0 No 48715 is way off the beaten track from its home shed at 8F Springs Branch Wigan as it labours away from Warwick and attacks Hatton bank with a train of low-loaders on 18th September 1965. To the right of No 48715 is the down relief line which ended at the summit at Hatton station, which once boasted three signalboxes — South, West and North, all now long gone. (T. R. Amos)

158) Bright sunshine envelopes the yard and massive coaling plant at 14B Kentish Town in 1959. Beneath the plant is Kentish Town *Jubilee* Class 4-6-0 No 45575 *Madras*, taking on fresh coal supplies in readiness for its next working. To the rear of *Madras* is an unidentified Class 5 4-6-0, whilst in the left of the picture on shed pilot duties is another Kentish Town inmate in the shape of Class 3F 'Jinty' 0-6-0T No 47241. (M. F. Higson — The Smokebox)

159) A 'foreigner' arrives at Nottingham (Midland) from the Sheffield area in the shape of LNER Thompson B1 Class 4-6-0 No 61111, a 41A Sheffield (Darnall) engine, at the head of an unknown express working (1E91) on 1st July 1961. Between February 1957 and June 1958. No 61111 had been at work on the Great Eastern section of the Eastern Region, at 30A Stratford and 30F Parkeston. It was withdrawn in September 1962 from Darnall. (D. K. Jones)

160) As Coventry shed had lost its allocation of locomotives as early as November 1958 engines had to be 'borrowed' from other depots. Ivatt Class 2 2-6-2T No 41231, from 84D Leamington is being employed on a parcels train at Coventry station on 12th January 1962 whilst the station was being rebuilt. Withdrawn from Leamington shed in May 1964, No 41231 was disposed of in the usual manner at Cashmores, Great Bridge. (D. K. Jones)

161) Although there is summer foliage to be seen in the foreground, the bleak looking hills in the background add a forbidding menace at Blea Moor during 1967. Having passed a distant signal at caution Class 8F 2-8-0 No 48703, from 55D Royston and fitted with a small snowplough, plods towards the camera with a lengthy freight train. By the end of 1967 regular steam workings were to cease over this route. (Mike Turner)

162) A maze of tracks and points at Wembley Central on 5th May 1962. Stanier Class 4 2-6-4T No 42470, a resident of 1A Willesden, steams into the station with a Euston to Wembley Cup Final local. This was the last F. A. final that No 42470 was to participate in for it was condemned in October of this year becoming yet another victim of the cutter's torch at Cashmores, Great Bridge, in February 1963. (B. W. L. Brooksbank)

163) A lone Class 5 'Caprotti' 4-6-0 No 44748 in steam, surrounded by diesels, in the running shed of its home base at 9A Longsight (Manchester) needs some form of attention on 12th April 1964, as indicated by the 'Not To Be Moved' notice attached to a lamp bracket. The shed was well into the transition period of changing from steam to diesel and No 44748 was withdrawn from there in September 1964. (D. K. Jones)

164) At dusk on 14th June 1965 LMS Class 5 4-6-0 No 44734, from 9D Newton Heath, curves away from Bolton Junction, Blackburn with the 18.15 Colne to Stockport parcels train. This was always a heavy loading which taxed its motive power to the full on the long climb to Sough Tunnel. This locomotive, a longstanding inmate of Newton Heath, finally succumbed to the inevitable in December 1967. (H. L. Holland)

165) Two unidentified Class 8F 2-8-0's accompany BR Class 4 2-6-0 No 76095, a visitor to 2D Banbury from 2J Aston, on 13th June 1965. Built in 1957, No 76095 was sent to Scotland in August of that year being allocated to 67A Corkerhill (Glasgow). After a spell at 65C Parkhead in 1961 it returned to Corkerhill and in September 1964, for reasons best known to the authorities it was drafted to 2E Saltley, in Birmingham. (Terry Ward)

166) During the fifties and early sixties the 55A Leeds (Holbeck) *Royal Scot* Class 4-6-0's were fully employed on former Midland rails to St. Pancras and St. Enoch on top expresses. By September 1961 they had been replaced by diesels and had been transferred away but for a six month period from June 1962 some returned to Holbeck, like No 46145 *The Duke of Wellington's Regt. (West Riding)* seen at Nottingham Midland on an express in August 1962. (G. W. Sharpe)

167) Stanier Class 4 2-6-4T No 42589 (8F Springs Branch Wigan) heads up the hill out of Wigan Wallgate station with the 11.55 am (Saturdays Only) Southport to Rochdale local passenger train on 22nd August 1964. Here, the ex. Lancashire & Yorkshire lines run alongside the West Coast Main Line at North Western station for a short distance, before diverging eastwards toward Bolton and Manchester. (H. L. Holland)

168) The pioneer member of the *Coronation* Class 4-6-2's No 46220 *Coronation*, based at 12B Carlisle (Upperby) stands in steam in the shed yard at 1B Camden with its impending replacement on 22nd June 1962. Once of 66A Polmadie (Glasgow), this 1937 built engine, once streamlined, served from August 1958 at 5A Crewe (North — twice and Upperby — twice), before being condemned from the latter in April 1963. It was scrapped at Crewe. (D. K. Jones)

169) A view of the inside of the half roundhouse at 5A Crewe (North) on 12th March 1959. A Class 5 4-6-0 is on the turntable and facing it is an unidentified BR Class 5 4-6-0 and *Coronation* Class 4-6-2 No 46249 *City of Sheffield*, a local Pacific. *City of Sheffield*, along with sister engine No 46242 *City of Glasgow*, helped to reverse the trend of 4-6-2's heading south from 66A Polmadie (Glasgow) by moving there in March 1961. (D. K. Jones)

170) Whilst cows grazed unconcerned in the nearby field, BR *Britannia* Class 4-6-2 No 70023 *Venus*, in a quite atrocious external condition, from 5B Crewe (South), heads northwards over Brock troughs, north of Preston, on 22nd July 1966, picking up fresh water supplies at the head of a fitted freight bound for Carlisle. Three months later and *Venus* was transferred to its final shed at 12A Carlisle (Kingmoor). (H. L. Holland)

171) The all but deserted platforms at Harlech are swathed in bright sunshine but there is a heavy mist hanging over the hills in the background on 17th July 1964. Ivatt Class 2 2-6-0 No 46520, a 6F Machynlleth locomotive, is in charge of the 1.17 pm stopping train to Barmouth. No 46520 was drafted to 5E Nuneaton in January 1965, moving on to 5D Stoke in June 1966 when the latter closed. It ended its days at 8E Northwich. (R. Picton)

172) A view at the Euston end of Birmingham (New Street) station before the diesels came. A group of spotters and a curious little girl and her father gather on the platform near to *Jubilee* Class 4-6-0 No 45555 *Quebec* (3B Bushbury — Wolverhampton) which is paired with a smaller capacity Fowler tender on 14th May 1957. *Quebec* is in charge of a Wolverhampton (High Level) to Euston express. (G. H. Wilson)

173) Another 3B Bushbury engine, Stanier Class 5 4-6-0 No 45310 lifts its safety valves at Clifton with a down fitted freight on 2nd April 1957. This type of train was the fore-runner to today's modern container trains — railfreight. No 45310 remained at Bushbury until April 1965, moving on to 2J Aston and then to Nuneaton during 1965. Withdrawal came in August 1968, from 10A Carnforth. (R. Butterfield)

174) A fire-iron, a shovel, piles of discarded ash and other bric-a-brac litter the shed yard at 14B Kentish Town on 14th June 1958. Two local 'Jinty' Class 3F 0-6-0 Tanks Nos 47200 (minus front numberplate) and No 47283 stand bunker to bunker. Peeping out from behind No 47200, which is fitted with condensing apparatus, is Hughes Class 6P5F 'Crab' 2-6-0 No 42721, from 27B Aintree, in Liverpool. (A. Swain)

175) A virtually brand new BR Class 4 2-6-4T No 80046, from 15D Bedford, pauses at Mill Hill, between Elstree and Hendon, with an up Bedford to St. Pancras local passenger on 3rd October 1953. By January 1957 this engine was based at 26A Newton Heath, being sent to 24E Blackpool. In May 1960 it moved to Scotland being allocated to 67A Polmadie (Glasgow) eventually being withdrawn from there in May 1967. (R. Butterfield)

176) The 12.07 pm Manchester (Central) to Glazebrook stopping passenger train pulls into Flixton station on 26th August 1952. It is being hauled by one of the first series of 'Director' Class 4-4-0's (LNER D10 Class) No 62653 *Sir Edward Frazer,* which has a train of LNER pattern carriages in tow. The GCR influence on CLC passenger stock can be seen by comparing the body profiles of the first two carriages, the second being a Robinson design. (Peter Hay)

177) We depart from BR STEAMING ON THE LONDON MIDLAND REGION — Volume 3 with two memories of yester-year from a slightly different viewpoint. The first is a view of the signalbox and small locomotive shed at Coniston, as photographed on 5th April 1957. (R. Butterfield)

MIDLAND RAILWAY
NOTICE TO DRIVERS, FIREMEN, AND ALL CONCERNED.

STOP.

ALL ENGINES REQUIRING TO ENTER THE SHED MUST BE BROUGHT TO A STAND AT THIS BOARD.

APRIL 1922.   **BY ORDER.**

178) A collectors item now but still in use then — A Midland Railway enginemens notice at 18A Toton shed on Sunday, 12th August 1956. (J. D. Gomersall)